FROM
LONELINESS
TO LOVE

Other Books by James Kavanaugh

FROM LONELINESS TO LOVE

James Kavanaugh

PERENNIAL LIBRARY

Harper & Row, Publishers, San Francisco

Cambridge, Hagerstown, New York, Philadelphia, Washington
London, Mexico City, São Paulo, Singapore, Sydney

FIRST HARPER & ROW PAPERBACK EDITION 1988

Illustrated by Alan Mazzetti

Library of Congress Cataloging-in-Publication Data
Kavanaugh, James J.
  From loneliness to love.
    1. Social isolation. 2. Loneliness. 3. Love.
I. Title.
HM291.K33   1986   302.5′45   86-45016
ISBN 0-06-250449-5 (cloth)
ISBN 0-06-250452-5 (paperback)

---

88 89 90 91 92   FG   10 9 8 7 6 5 4 3 2 1

to those who have known the pain
of loneliness and have
endured to discover love
and
to offer comfort to those who
are hanging on in faith,
still believing that their
deliverance will come

especially to those special few
whose unconditional love
has rescued me
from a devouring loneliness

INTRODUCTION

Loneliness is the painful, relentless destroyer of human life. Curiously it doesn't seem to matter whether one lives alone or with others, whether one is rich or poor, ambitious or passive. But serenity and enthusiasm do matter, and so do communication and contact—and especially gratitude and a love of life—for the ultimate antidote to loneliness is love.

Acute loneliness is not reserved for the aged, but can strike the young and middle-aged as well. Some fortunate ones have never really known it. Most of us have. It may occur after a divorce or a geographical move, after a death, the breakup of a romance, or the loss of a job. Or especially with low feelings of self-worth and when life loses its meaning. It often comes with overwork or burnout, and although medication and rest can help, love is the ultimate cure.

It can be the love of a child or grandchild, a new and fulfilling romance, an exciting job that brings us into contact with new people. Or as often it can be our deep enjoyment of the ocean and forests, the fields and mountains, or a simple garden. It usually is whatever vision brings energy into our lives and wipes away the bland and lonely existence that seems pointless. It ends when love again pervades our life.

To move from loneliness to love usually means to take a risk and create the kind of personal environment and support system we need. For some this is not difficult.

Their personalities and self-confidence are such that life is soon vital again no matter the stress or conflict. For others it is far more traumatic—for the timid and diffident, the self-conscious and shy, those whose self-love is fragile and who find it hard to reach out and give or accept love.

Ultimately the move from loneliness to love is the move from self-absorption to a broad and vital vision of life. Loneliness may reveal to us that a way of life which has been effective for us for years no longer works. To escape loneliness does not necessarily require the perfect love relationship, though millions believe that is the only way. It begins with a light in our own heart, a spark reflected in our own eye, a sense of gratitude for what we have and are and not a narrow focus on what is missing in our lives.

If I am lonely, and I often am, it is because I do not make the move to do anything about it. Sometimes I feel almost powerless to do so when my energy is concentrated on survival. With patience and courage we move past this point, reach out and discover that the seeds of loneliness, like the seeds of serenity and love, rest in our own hearts. And the move from loneliness to love is our own choice— perhaps the most significant one we make. For if life is not joy and peace and love, it is nothing at all.

This book is about the deep pain of loneliness and the healing power of love. It is for those like myself who have felt the sense of separation from life and love—sometimes for no logical reason and for too long a time. It is above all a book of reassurance and hope as well, recognizing that by courage and patience and determination, loneliness *can dissolve into love like the cold greyness of early morning melts into the warm splendor of dawn.*

James Kavanaugh
Laguna Beach,
California

Of Love and Loneliness

I have walked down enough silent streets,
Lost in the shadows of my own consciousness,
Afraid to love lest I lose the fantasies
    that never really came true,
Afraid to surrender lest I lose some control
    I never really wanted,
Glancing from left to right in hope that joy
    and freedom would envelop me.

Loneliness became a gradual companion
    when I had not really known him before,
And choice terrified me lest I be
    only like everyone else,
Which in truth was all I ever wanted to be.
To love myself should be nourishment enough,
    according to the wise and self-contained,
But for me it never seemed so from childhood.
Neither was admiration or the embrace
    of loving strangers.

It was not beauty I sought
    in some current cultural vogue,
But a heart which touched mine, captured mine,
    clung to mine at its very core and drew me
        as powerfully to love in turn.
Forever it seems I sought one to love
    without a backlog of private hurt and pain,

Without the invading fog that would somehow
	mar our love and make it human.

Such never came and I searched the books
	that told me what rightfully should be mine.
As time passed I feared I might not love at all
And the nourishment not given in childhood
	might be lost forever.
When I did not want to live without such love and
	seemed incapable of enduring the pain others
		silently bear,
I traded loneliness for love, fragile, feeble, afraid,
But locked in my will and my heart:
	To see as well as to be seen,
	To listen as well as to be heard.

Love was not what I had been told or
	what others projected upon me,
But my private gift which promised
	to grow every day,
And slowly the loneliness lifted
	beyond anything money or power could buy.
Now I am a man among men, loving
	far more rationally and willfully
	than I knew could exist,
In the massive, enduring, most significant
	struggle of all,
		that of loneliness and love.

The Lonely Mornings

The lonely mornings wake before dawn
When memories cascade from childhood and faces
    seep from the grave,
Or emerge from a remote and buried past.
Voices long silent drift in the wind
    to love and accuse,
And I wonder if I have ever really seen anyone
    or understood clearly any pain but my own.
I want to rise above my wounded flesh
    and scarred brain,
Rise above bruised emotions and the debris
    of personal failure,
And open my arms and heart to the world,
    to nourish each friend who needs my strength
And transform each secret enemy
    into one I can again love.
There are no triumphs anymore
    that remain triumphant.
Beetles and daffodils, hummingbirds and lilacs
    mean more than any power
        or seeming success.
Sex without love is finally drained of all comfort,
And the most sophisticated competition is but a
    child's tantrum on an ancient playground.
What is life if not laughter and love,
    caring and compassion,
        fresh bread and crisp radishes?

It is time to tear down the prisons
        without walls or bars,
The lives without meaning, the frenetic motion
        that is only a flight from madness,
To embrace the night, the sunset,
        the rain and gentle breezes,
And to love above all else the lonely mornings
        that wake before dawn.

Finally I Understand

Finally I understand the loss of you
    and why I am shattered at your departure.
No one ever loved me like you, cared as much,
    gave as much, asked as little.
        No one ever looked at me as you did.
You were the harbor where I came home,
    a boat in a bathtub made to feel
        like a multi-masted schooner.
I do not know what to do without you.
    I cannot replace your eyes, your smile,
        your joy in my presence.
This very moment I want no one but you,
    to hear your voice, to feel the reassurance
        that only you can give.
And all the while you lived, I had no idea
    you held the pieces together.
Now I am a broken statue,
    a mortally wounded soldier waiting to die.
    Where did you go?
        Where are you resting now?
I would take you as a barely breathing corpse,
    a paraplegic, my God, a silent vegetable,
And love you as much as anyone in the world
    ever loved, because finally I understand.

What does one do with grief that never leaves,
    the kind that time cannot heal?
How does one live when sadness is everywhere
    at your departure?
I scream silently for you in the night,
    long for you each morning,
Your wisdom and kindness, your generosity
    and strength, most of all, your love,
Uncomplaining, unjudging, you held my heart
    and made me feel that the whole world stopped
        to stare at me.
Perhaps I loved you too much, and you me,
    but I want to go where you are,
      breathe where you breathe,
      see what you see.
But now I live in exile, ignorant of an adventure I
    cannot share when we shared
    everything before,
Wondering if I can ever love anyone
    as much as you loved me,
Afraid I cannot feel as free and strong
    in anyone's presence again.
I wish I had asked you how to love,
    for I cannot open my heart completely,
      to love without question or qualification,
And I fear that no one but you can really teach me.
At times, near the end, I thought you wanted
    to die, that you were afraid to live.

Now I know that you loved with your whole being
   and death had lost its power in love.
What more is life than this? And finally I
   understand.

Why Do I Love You?

Why do I love you?
There are no words, only familiar smells
    and closeness beyond all reckoning.
Mind reaching mind, heart surrendering to heart,
A gentle touch in the night, a quiet look of love
    On a grey afternoon.
If there is more, I know not what it is,
For fictional love has become a lonely dance
    Where I sit on the sidelines
And watch the untroubled lovers pair up
    and walk away.
I never wanted perfection, only caring,
Not striking beauty, but honest understanding,
One who simply knows me and loves me
    for what I am,
    And has ceased to look for anyone else,
Not because there is no time,
    but no possible reason.
I want time with you, an arm to lean on
    when mine is weary.
I know what all the books say
    and the current, cultural vogue
    Of strong and independent men and women,
Walking side by side
    without intrusion or interference,
    Well content with a partner
        or satisfied without one.

I am not so strong and doubt I will ever be, for the
ego
That kept me raw and alone has given way to
reality.
I still want to nurture and be nurtured, to care
about each need,
To be concerned about each pain and to know
there is one
Who lives to make my days joyful, to bring my
heart and hope alive.
Keep your fierce and triumphant
independence,
Your sterile partnerships, your separate lives of
vaunted strength!
I am often but a fragile child, knowing that
you are as well.
If I need a part-time mother, and you a part-time
father,
Thus it is despite masks and appearances and
will ever be,
And I will trade it for all the rigid independence in
the world.

Milton

Milton feels much better without sugar or caffeine,
    Without red meat, salt, alcohol, or nicotine.
Now that his blood pressure is perfect,
He jogs twice a day and he can hit a backhand
    straight down the line
Now that he skis, surfs, and swims
    the backstroke,
    He has only one remaining problem.
He's got to find a reason to live!

All These Years

All these years not aware
    of a young boy's abandonment,
All of his energies channeled
    to gain love through accomplishment,
Facing the intellectual challenges
    with a mind tense for battle,
Facing the physical challenges
    with a body taut against pain,
Ignoring the scars of heart and soul
    that never appeared on the surface
Until they emerged all at once
    to destroy his life.
How he hung on is an unrecorded miracle,
When all the facile skills
    that once proved effective
Now were coldly denied him.
It was as if his face were distorted
    and unloveable,
His body sexless and helpless
    and ravaged by open wounds.
His very being an unwanted thing
    because he gave his power away
To those, as wounded as he,
    who only knew how to love him badly.
Yet, he hung on, not knowing why,
    trying desperately to reawaken the past
When joy filled his very soul.
    And each day a step closer to fulfillment.

But the past would not return
    and the future came but one hour at a time.
So he clings to each hour, taking the steps
    he feared to take a lifetime ago.

You and I

You and I could be the greatest
    lovers, could abandon hurt to the wind,
Could make of life the paradise
    it was meant to be.
But even you and I have drawn
    the shades on whom we really are,
Afraid that the very revelation
    will make love and longing impossible,
When in reality,
    it is love's only chance.

Lately

Lately the mountains look sadly at me
    Because I do not hear their eternal song,
And the patient palms frown
    when I ignore their whispering.
I want to lie on the moor, on the desert sand,
    And let the night cover me,
        the earth reclaim me
Because in the torment of spirit and madness
    disguised as wisdom,
I did not listen to the inner melody
    which directs all creatures.
Who walk the earth and flow from its core.
I would have made a nice bumblebee,
A superb peony, a wondrous apple tree,
I've only failed as a man.
There is time to plant all over again
And as I live, to seem much more like a rosebush
Than a man, more like a brook
    winding its way through rocks,
Than a conqueror stomping his way
    across the earth.
Watch the birds, the trees, the disappearing sun,
    the laughing dawn, the rattling
        and splashing waters.
They will tell you more of life than all the masters—
    Without ego or interference—
    without pretense or projection—
Only in simple, rhythmic, pulsing,
    liberating truth!

The Guys

The guys gathered one evening
    to talk about women,
        How they'd been defaced
            and disgraced by them
And left holding their limp manhood
    in their hands,
        How you couldn't trust 'em anymore
And had to learn to live without 'em no matter
    How long it took or how hard it was.
They bitched about the single life as well,
    How it bankrupted you with trips
        and costly dinners
Almost as fast as marriage did
    With kids and furniture and costly houses.
They agreed to a man that women were stronger,
    Better organized and quicker to recover,
And found support in everything
    from sewing quilts
    To a new recipe for quiche or lasagna.
Then it grew quiet—though they wondered about
    the guy
        Who didn't show up because he needed
            his weekly ration of sex.
Then another guy left early
    because he had planned
        A costly dinner with a costly lady
And he had to protect his investment at all costs.

The rest of the group wondered about a dance
     on Friday
And if there would be any new ladies around.

It Won't Be Long

Well, it won't be long and I'll be free again,
    Free to brush the leaves of trees
        Like the fingers of forgotten friends.
    Free to sprawl across the rocks
        Like a familiar bed too long forgotten.
Too long I've been held in a prison
    of my own creation,
    Trapped and abandoned by fears
        of solitude and loneliness.
Too many voices have demanded,
    too many hands have grasped,
    Too many crowds have held me captive.
But it won't be long and I'll be free again:
    I feel the raging torrent in my brain,
    The north wind like vertigo in my stomach,
    The summer fog along the ocean
        blinding my eyes.
All the warning signs that scream for release,
All the haunting cries of boyhood that lure me
    To wander in my private forest
    where no path is unfamiliar
    no bird or flower is a stranger.
I know the rusted railroad track that bridges the
    Little Swamp,
The rushes that house frogs and guard
    water snakes from intruders.

I am one of them, a stranger only
    where the traffic is too loud,
    Voices too insistent, grasping hands
        too demanding.
And I would assuredly die of emptiness
    if I didn't know
    That it won't be long and I'll be free again.

I Go Where I Cannot See

I go where I cannot see and see where I cannot go,
People are wonderful, people are dreadful,
They give life and hasten death,
Talk of nothing, offer me hope and love.
I cannot bear another margarita and empty laugh,
    Not a single hors d'oeuvre and silver tray,
Not another story or eyes that look beyond me
      To wonder what I do and what my income is,
        If I am significant enough to chat with.
Am I the only one who is trying
    to create another world?
The problem is a simple one. I did what I was told
    for so long
      That I have dulled my own inner voice
        that echoes endlessly in confusion.
Is family the only way to go, children
    waiting for dinner,
    Or one more trip to Disneyland?
I only want a port in some storm,
    a place to weep and wonder,
A voice that says nothing, a heart
      that asks nothing but my presence.
Am I the only one who does not know how to live?
I am still in school following the schedule
    for class and recess and meals.
My God! Let me go! Let me run free!
      Let me babble like a decent brook,
And roar like any respectable ocean!
Who made me like I am, child and nomad,

Vagabond and lover of the hearth, rebel and patriot
    Who ignores the morning news
        and pursues the setting sun?
Where is the home for the man who has none?
Where is the orbit vast enough, the universe
           wild enough, the stars close enough?
I want a friend who understands, whose arm
    is linked in mine,
      Whose vision penetrates and words
        somehow touch my soul.
How often must I begin again?

No World for You

This is no world for you
With its abrasions and harshness,
Its greed and anger and desperation,
Its loneliness and weariness and pain.
You were made for another life
Where children play as adults
    and adults as children,
Where brutality and coldness are words unknown
And soothing, gentle words and touches
Have the same esteem as power and arrogance
    in our present world.
I see you wrapped in golden light
    and hold you there.
I see the tenderness of your mind,
    the silkiness of your feelings,
And send you nothing but love
    from a planet far beyond our own.
You are my friend, and only your image
    must change to survive.
You and I are right counting stars
    and plucking blades of grass—
They are all wrong in pursuit
    of neutral strangulation.
When it is all over, only love and flowers
    really count, laughter and honesty,
        beauty and caring—
So let us begin today and live on our own planet
    with our own people—as long as is destined—
        and know

That beyond anger and pride, castles and cars,
    we have more than all the rest—
    our love—our silence—and a vision of a world
    of total innocence and quiet joy.

The Only Sanity

The only sanity left is madness,
    madness enough to resist all
    that is respectable and decent.

I stand among the lonely
    at their luaus and cocktails,
Hear the stories I've heard before,
    study the strong men's faces
    and see the dullness of their eyes,
Endure the silent pain
    of docile and obedient wives.
I watch niceness replace passion
    and fear give birth to sterile kindness.
What is there left to be proud of?
    A yard without weeds?
    A car without scratches?
What remains to boast of?
    Money in the bank?
    A computer that finally tells you how to live?
Sometimes I wish life were a deck of cards
That had to be reshuffled every few years.
    Blacks would be married to whites,
    Salesmen would be nuclear physicists,
    Astronauts would be chimney sweeps
    And chimney sweeps would be surgeons.
    Poets would be bartenders and lawyers poets,
    Skinny women would be fat and fat women
        men.

Old men would be boys, and young women
would be frightened matrons.
All at the turn of a card, the shuffle of a deck,
And life would be wild and crazy and alive again.

Man-Child

Beyond plans of success and dreams of affluence,
Beyond threats and boasts
    and seeming confidence,
I see your fear and know
    that when you lose your boyhood
    You lose all that makes you warm
        and attractive as a man.
Life is not lived in spurts
    where manhood destroys boyhood
    Like some major surgery never to be undone.
It is not your obvious triumphs
    and heady expertise,
    But the laughing, playful, awkward boy in you
        we love,
That spontaneous, unpredictable part
    that can drop everything
    To hear a distant seal trumpeting
        on the midnight rocks,
Or watch the messy, nervous swallow
    building his mortared nest
    And fouling picture windows and garage
        doors
        like a bad mason.
When the boy is gone, the man is all
    drive and head,
    Without arms and legs,
    Without eyes and ears and energy
        And some intrinsic joy.

There is no victory as beautiful as spontaneity
    and passion,
No success that can match
    the vibrant feeling of life,
    And assuredly,
No one more beautiful than a man
    who moves relentlessly and bravely
    Beyond the hungry, desperate needs
        of childhood,
And still remains in daily, loving contact
    with the boy.

Certain

She was certain
I would ask her to bed,
Manipulate and seduce,
Try almost anything
    to reduce her to soap opera,
        Lady Chatterley helplessness.
After all I was a man,
    Prototypical of all the men
She had read about and seen on TV
Carrying my gonads in my hand,
Ready to strew my seed like sand
On any victimized, unliberated female.
Unaware that I was as masculinist
    as she feminist,
As frightened of closeness, as wary
    Of my space and protective of my inner grace,
The only, trusted guardian of my own soul.
We ate and talked and then grew silent,
Walked and watched the tiled houses
    climb the mountains,
Wondered about angels and told
    our well-rehearsed hero stories.
I did not touch her hand nor fantasize her breast,
As grateful as she for my own privacy,
And proud to be a man that just laid to rest
    the legacy of some distorted male history—
Content to be a life upon the earth, a mystery still
    unsolved
        By all the self-appointed critics of my sex.

There Are Days

There are days when I could run for president,
Direct General Motors in the morning
    and Chrysler in the afternoon,
When I could thrill an audience of ten thousand,
And walk hand in hand
    with the most prestigious leaders on earth,
When my conversation sparkles
    and my imagination is in overdrive.
When I could be loved by starlets
    and international beauties,
Create elaborate stories for the stage or screen,
Wander from country to country
    at home in every land,
Solving political conflicts that have endured
    for centuries,
And healing the wounds of starving children
    and despairing adults.

And there are days when emerging from bed
    seems impossible,
When a barking dog or cooing dove
    can drive me quite mad,
When taking a shower and fixing cornflakes
    is a major undertaking,
And taking my car in to repair a wiper blade
    a complex enterprise,
When I could not shine shoes
    or run a hot-dog stand,

And I tremble at the thought
    of saying "Hello" to the postman,
When the cleaning lady is bored by my dialogue,
And no woman in her right mind
    would give me time for lunch,
When to leave the living room frightens me
    beyond endurance,
And I could not create a story
    for a high school paper.

The miracle is that on either kind of day,
Your eyes still gaze at me as if no one else walks
    the earth,
And your smile forever says, "I love you
    no matter what."
Then General Motors means not nearly as much
    As the tears we shed on the living room floor,
    Or the sunset we share in serenity and silence.

Stubby

Stubby has more confidence with less reason than
    anyone I've ever known,
He's thirty pounds overweight,
    works ten hours a week,
    Spends more time traveling than the pope,
And he's as comfortable with a beggar
    as a diplomat
On an exclusive tennis court, he wore khaki pants,
    three-dollar shoes, and a Hawaiian shirt,
    returned maybe ten balls in two sets
    and told me later he thinks his game
        is getting stronger.
He laughs at everything, eats what he wants,
    and will break any appointment.
His family background is gravied with everything
    from alcoholic parents to child abuse
        and total neglect.
His saga reads like a TV documentary on how lives
    are destroyed.
While I worry and wonder and check my psyche
    assiduously,
    he picks up grateful ladies
        at assorted night spots
He would play golf with Arnold Palmer without
    embarrassment
        and shoot 162,
    sing at a bar, though he's totally tone deaf,
    and dance with anyone
        always using the same two-step shuffle.

He contradicts everything I've ever read in
   theology, psychology, and anthropology.
Either he's got the damndest genes
Or he's the one successful lobotomy that left
   everything but gloom, fear, and insecurity
      intact.
If that's the case, I'm looking for the same doctor!

I Have Tried

I have tried a thousand times to say "goodbye,"
To drift across the prairies in search
    of some nomadic life
    Which promised the freedom
        that lonely men write about.
I have scoured deserts and wandered
    through the neon lights
    Of every city with character and promise
        and new energy.
But never could I forget you, your face,
    your body huddled next to mine
        in promise committed forever,
Your loyalty, your readiness to listen
    and to talk far into the night.
We have tried so many times
    that Columbus would have turned back
    And Cortez would been content
        to write fantasies and fables.
What are life and relationships?
    What is compromise
    And what is mere reality?
No one really made me happier than you,
No one offered me more adventure and gentleness
    and freedom.
I have known my moments of passing ecstasy
    with strangers,
    Known the smell of the Orient
        and monuments of Europe.

I have felt the sea on my face
       and the promise of love
       Looming just around the corner of any street.
But I always returned to you,
       not because you were the most beautiful,
       Though your caramel eyes
              always looked directly and lovingly at me.
All you asked was love and commitment
       and for that you promised
Every effort to fulfill every dream, every
       moment to hear each cry.
Lately it has occurred to me as I study
       relationships and count
       The assorted memories of my life
              that you gave more than anyone.
We had our storms, though perhaps not enough,
       our explorations,
       Though assuredly not as much as we needed.
But beyond all we had a yearning to know life,
       To love each other,
       To care beyond all words
              and to share the secrets
That most keep to themselves
       in some sacred, lonely silence.
Now that I finally know I will not live forever,
       I wonder
       What more the gods offer anyone
              who treads the earth.

I would like finally to care for you,
to watch your dreams unravel,
And to look far beyond the narrow vision
of my own horizons.
Finally I think I can, I must,
if life is to mean anything at all,
And the reason I could not finally
say "goodbye"
Was that some power beyond all reckoning
had bound us in this life
Or in the last, and we are only
a loving destiny
Proving that human love can grow,
survive, forgive, and start anew
Until it is as close to God
as a man of earth can come.

Still the Same Boy

I am still the same boy walking
    alone in the woods,
Batting stones for hours
    because no one ever listened—
And only a rare and exquisite friend listens now—
Therapists listen to their own memories
    and fantasies,
Even lovers cease listening so I
       cease talking about my reality
Because I am not heard.
I have only one story to tell,
The same one I have tried to tell all my life,
But who wants to hear it?
Thus we talk to ourselves
And even the best relationships
    are filled with holes,
Not the baring and sharing of souls.
What tragedy! To live a whole life
    and not be known
Even by ourselves, and rarely by others.
The sensitive ones feel the pain
    and loneliness, unable finally
       to steel themselves against it,
And die prematurely.
Most do not even try, and yet the only healing
    is in being heard,
Really heard, and the caring is in the hearing.

So I walk the woods and bat my stones
    and vainly hope
For one lover who would finally hear and heal
    what nothing or no one else can!

Marcia

Well, Marcia made it to the top
    and men take orders from her now
    Like docile little boys looking for mothers.
So she's not angry anymore,
    all her perks are in place,
    And she has the Jaguar she always dreamed of
As well as the deluxe condo with the Jacuzzi
    in the patio.
There is nothing she can't buy,
    nowhere she can't go,
    No one her portfolio would not impress.
She finally has it all—except love
    and a reason to live.
So she often sits silently at night, watching TV
    And sipping only the very best wines,
Until she drifts off, remembering
    when she could laugh
    At a beach barbecue and make love
        in a meadow,
And wakes up wondering how to find her way
    back down
    To all the things she lost
        fighting her way to the top.

You Reached Out!

You reached out beyond all the rest
Saw the fear and clouded power
And knew I must be rescued from drowning
    in my own self-created ocean.
Others wished me well, made suggestions,
    told me their own stories of survival and success,
Chided me, prodded me, challenged me,
    accused me, but did not understand the child
        struggling still to be a man.
You would not give up, sent by God
    as His most unlikely messenger
And drew me from the depths
    that you had once known yourself.
I will not forget your love,
    Your assurance that "Nothing's Easy"—
    Your quiet recitation of your own hidden pain.
Now I understand your success, your energy,
    your courage,
    Because your reached out
        Beyond all the rest!

Boats Waiting

Fishing boats waiting patiently at dawn
   on the shore, creaking and stretching
      from too short a night,
The eastern sky grey and vermillion
   above the mountains,
Low clouds lined like the living and the dead
   expecting judgment.
The Sea of Cortez, still and placid,
   awaiting new explorers of the spirit
      to give fresh meaning to the land.
Mexican fishermen readying their nets,
   laughing and chattering endlessly
      like restless children
With no philosophical questions unanswered,
   their task appointed, lives outlined,
      and babies still a delight.
Existence as clear as that of the boats
   mingling work and play.
The dorado wait, the pompano and grouper
   and helpless lobsters,
And the confident tourists who hire the boats
   or lie in the sun, planning a release
      from the prison time and fear have built.

The light creeps slowly across the water,
    softly across the sky,
Giving a burst of color to the surrounding
    mountains
            and the now lapping, stirring sea.
A gentle breeze eases heat still present from
    yesterday's torturous sun.
Was this the time Christ walked by,
    as sleepless and full of dreams as I,
Hoping to transform a struggling world
    into love and understanding?
War and hate are unthinkable
    in the pre-dawn fragility,
            even as the fishermen's voices grow louder.
The soft purring of an engine,
    the light now assuredly of the day,
The breeze stronger, birds blinking
    and chirping their way to life,
The grass huts on the shore
    ready to protect the morning lovers
        when fear is most vulnerable
        and dreams most unfulfilled.
The sky changes so softly,
    so do the mountains and the water,
    All the victims of the light's enlightenment
        even as am I.

This is the free and glorious time for me when
    nothing is expected
    save bare consciousness and gentle perceptions.

The fishermen are gone and I am alone
    with the morning light
And the friendly, gasping, startled lisping
    of the waves.
Life began here so many times
    and mine begins here now,
Childhood scars not yet totally dissolved,
    painful echoes of my last love
        still too discordant to begin again.
I wait like Adam in his paradise, too long alone,
    and bid the God of sea and sky
        to create my own Eve,
            mother of all the living.
To see her slip from the rose silhouette of the sky,
    stride eagerly over the distant mountains,
Swim the Sea of Cortez and emerge naked
    in the shallow waters, knowing even as I do,
        instinctively and immediately
That, at God's own bidding,
    I am for her and she is for me.

Then to begin life at the start,
    knowing all we know, loving all we love,
Afraid only of isolation and ambition
    and fear itself,
Afraid of losing the eloquence of this soft morning.
Disappearing together into a grass hut
    to make gentle, slow,
    silent, and spiritual love,
Promising only that together we will try
    to make sense of it all,

Until we join the same morning skies,
    floating like clouds with those
        who have gone before and will come after,
Bathing in the same sea and sharing
    the same soft light.
Aware that we have only this day, this hour,
    this moment, but aware that it is enough,
Because we have it all to ourselves,
    forever!

I Wonder

I wonder about the writers
    who create the afternoon soaps,
Where passion lasts for decades
    and elderly men are dashing,
Husbands divorce or bring flowers and wives sigh
    Or find passion in their dentists' arms.
The good are so good, the villains so villainous,
    And nice guys not only finish last,
        but are finished off.
I imagine a lonely old lady writing her socks off
    Or an isolated old man
        trying to get even with life
    For all the rotten tricks it played on him.
Finally there is revenge and inverted history
    With the twist of a computer for lonely viewers
Who devour the suave lovers and curse the fiends
    To refurbish a life that has grown dull
        and unexciting,
And can hardly wait until tomorrow
    when Martin meets
    The miserably married Minerva
        in a dark parking lot
And ravishes her to new ecstacy
        in the back seat of his rented Lincoln,
Even as he plans to spend the same night
    with her sister-in-law in his rented cabin.

And the transfixed viewers could care less,
    longing to meet Martin,
    Only to discover that he wears a toupee,
And has been impotent
    since his wife left him for a bus driver.

To Moya

In the days of covered wagons
    and stubborn mule trains
    Making their way across the desert
        in hostile territory,
You above all would have survived the drought,
    the baking heat,
    The blinding sand, washed-out trails
    and flash floods.
You would have consoled
    the lonely and frightened children,
    Comforted the dying wives
        and nursed the desolate babies.
You would have made strong men stronger
    and faint hearts stalwart,
    Grubbed for food and water
        when none was to be found.
In another age the frontier would have stood
    at attention
    And kissed your shadow as it passed
        in the moonlight.
Each death would have broken your wounded heart
    to weeping,
    Even as your face would have revealed
        only the courage to go on.
Each wagon interred in mud and despair
    would at your command
    Have made another, fiercer, final effort
        to push ahead.

Your pain would have remained hidden,
    your scars concealed,
        Your laughter would have rung out victory
            in the teeth of defeat.
Your determination and drive would have been
    cursed by the timid,
        Your ancient wisdom and understanding
            mocked by the cowards,
Your love and compassion misunderstood
    by its very abundance.

And today, when the desert is silent
    and manageable,
        When the wagon trains are buried in sand
            and text books,
You still live and love with the lore and loyalty
    of the frontier,
        And fight like a mother mountain lion
            to save her cubs.
You will pay a price for your strength
    among the fainthearted,
        You will suffer silently with a heart beating
            in every direction
In a world where justice and compassion
    are silenced by greed,
        Where artifice and tyranny stand brazenly
            as power and virtue,
Where empty words are given the same currency
    as a hero's deeds.
        Thus, I am grateful that you are my dear and
            eternal friend,

And when I fear to move on, or tremble
   at the overriding enemy,
      I take comfort that you and I ride together
         side by side
In the same covered wagon.

Beyond Rough Edges

Beyond your harshness and rough edges
    lives warmth and comfort
        and gentle compassion.
At times I want to run
    from your righteousness and blind strength.
The hurts you hide under steel,
The memories of pain calcified and angry.
Then I take you in my arms and feel
    the pain dissolve, the memories disappear,
And I know if I love you enough,
    your softness and confidence
        will emerge to stay.
I love you beyond the hurt you impart,
Love you in some profound corner of my heart.
I would like you to be mine
    even as I fear what life has done
        to make you too angry to accept
An unconditional love.

Fear Stands Like a Dark Forest

Fear stands like a dark forest without a path
    to freedom,
        As I wander helplessly
            amid its foreboding presence.
Fear emerges like a dark, cold mountain,
    snow capped and formidable,
        As I stare hopelessly at its massive resistance.
Fear explodes like a roaring river,
    swollen and ripping at its banks,
        As I glance timidly at its unmeasured power.
Fear screams like all the assembled, fiery demons
    of the earth's core,
        As I look in terror at its devouring appetite.

Only courage remains, the least spark of David
    versus a gargantuan Goliath,
But as courage holds its ground
    —quietly, patiently, relentlessly,
        the trees slowly stand aside in the forest,
        the mountain silently bows its head,
        the river speaks more softly,
    the demons pause to listen,
And the fortitude of a feeble man, frightened,
    but determined,
        Makes his way to peace and serenity
            and a quiet victory
Over the most brutal and overwhelming fear.

I Wanted to Be

I wanted to be what I thought
    you expected me to be,
Or what others told me I could be,
Living on energy borrowed from years ahead
    And wondering if I was gaining on Emerson
      and Whitman.
The options were there—gathered like rats
    in a maze
Ready to scurry wherever the tasty pellets
    seemed more tempting.
When even the pellets weren't satisfying
    I knew I was in trouble,
    When vagrants on street corners
      seemed to have it more together
Than bankers and brokers and even movie stars,
    Certainly than me.
Now gradually I am content to be who I am,
    baby step by baby step,
      A scared kid from a small town,
        Well aware that I can only successfully
          be myself,
        Knowing that you love me
          for a whole different set of reasons
            than the magazine ads proclaim.
I feel the light flowing from my heart
    and the sadness of expectations
      slowly dissolving.

The vagrants now don't look better or worse
    than the bankers.
We all do it the way we can and consistent joy
    is worth all the recognition in the world.
Love is the answer to loneliness,
    beginning with the love of who I am,
And being who I am now and always
    is the greatest risk in the world.

I Cannot Answer

I cannot answer for all the others,
Nor understand their uncomplaining compliance
    With routine's demands
        and seeming boredom.
I know nothing of age or settling down,
Or boundaries established by history or custom.
Grey hair is no barrier or wrinkles,
Time spent or time remaining means nothing
    To a heart that requires freedom to live.
In another life I would have carried my tent
    Across the endless desert,
And sailed my creaking ship
    across an unknown sea.
Now I will wander freeways and crevices,
    Hear strange voices,
And make friends with whomever is at hand.
It is not a choice I made but a destiny I inherited,
Not a habit but an issue of blood and bone
    and madness.
Stand back from life and observe it carefully.
What makes sense and what is imprisonment?
Who knows consistent happiness and who follows
    A path made by docile ants,
Pursuing docile ants in prescribed procession.
I have no idea where I must live or how,
No blueprint made in Japan or heaven.
Only a heart and mind that know
    What is true and what is false,
    What feels good and what feels bad,
And assuredly I will not speak for all the others
    Who have no questions and no answers.

Undecided Man

Undecided man,
Afraid to surrender to nothingness,
Afraid as well to build a dream step by step,
Because the dreams of so many others
    get in the way,
Afraid to attack the day
    and chase the relentless demons away.
They gather in mobs and each one challenged
    Is replaced by two more,
As in the ancient tale of Herculean labors.
There is only one way, to walk alone,
    Step by step, and take the hands
That are offered without strangulation.
Your madness is your salvation,
The source and strength of each creation,
    Not backing off until you have faced the fear
        of death and failure, aging and fatigue.
Undecided man with decisions stretching across
        the night and day.
Only a silent, forward motion can drive
    the assembled terrors away.
Order is heaven's first law and yours as well,
And courage and forward motion will drive
        the raging demons back to hell.

Dearest Friend

Dearest friend, I know your pain,
 And have felt it for months
  in the crevices of my heart
   and the far reaches of my soul—
 Where I had never dared venture before.
I reach out to you across the miles,
 Touch you, hold you, understand your grief
  and the torment of your shadows.
 And more than this, I love you.
I have felt such pain
 When only death promised relief
  and no light shone
 Anywhere in eyes or on the earth.
Hang on, my friend, step by step,
 the beauty will return.
Hold on, beloved one, the days will reappear.
 Now the trees are black, the sky grey,
  And the flowers muted like dry grass.
Remember the songs you composed—
 the songs I play so often—
 The whispered words of love.
There is still life to live, more pure and real
 than before,
And there is love where once
 there was only clinging.
There is love, as if it never was before!

You Are Your Own Answer

You are your own answer,
Beyond books and seers,
psychics or doctors
Beyond the strength that comes
from what you have accomplished.
Your weakness is as valuable as your strength,
Your helplessness as loveable as your charm.
You are God's child and each step of the way,
He gives you bread and not a stone,
food and not a serpent.
All is part of the plan, as you look within
And listen to the quiet, persistent voice
that tells you who you are.
There is no strength greater than yours.
No wisdom not available to you.
And love and light will flood your being
When you believe deeply enough to know
that you are your own answer
In the beauty and creativity that make us all one.
No one beyond our love, no one not connected.
Abandon anger and fear to the wind,
sadness and pseudo-strength to the earth.
Be who you are, in whatever state,
and you will discover
That you are your own answer
in the silence of your heart.
Where all light and power dwell forever.

Deep in the Dark of the Night

Deep in the dark of the night,
When children sweat and sleep,
And peaceful adults, with their lives in order,
    slumber gracefully,
I sit and wonder about my life, not morbidly,
    but like a spectator at a strange movie.
My parents, lovers, wives, friends, my work
    and the tragedies never expected.
I wonder how much I could have controlled,
How much I could have done differently,
Why my feelings leap to the surface of my being
    and are not hidden
        in some comforting defense.
There were years of confidence
    and endless ambition,
        dreams unnumbered and fantasies as elaborate
        as German castles on the Rhine.
Now life is simpler, but not simple enough
    to allow me to sleep.
It is in process, simplifying,
    and that would keep the hardiest awake.
Fears long buried have surfaced,
    deeds I want to do are left undone,
Friends I need at my side are scattered
    throughout the hemisphere.
Suddenly men and women I once thought
    commonplace
        are beautiful.

There is a healing only in claiming
    that what is mine is mine,
    madness as well as victories.
And the real courage is to continue on,
    Deep in the dark of the night.

I Long to Let Go

I long to let go,

To release all the illusions
    that separate me from what is,
To feel my body pulse and soar,
    lifting my mind from its fears,
And repairing all the ancient scars of my soul,
To float through the day and dance
    through the night,
Following the directions of winds and clouds
    And ever in touch with the heavens,
To feel my roots descend into the deep waters
    of the earth's core
        like a palm tree in the desert,
        Strong because it bends,
        Unafraid because it flows
           with water and life.
I am not the solid, unshaken, and venerable oak.
I am leaves flying from branches,
    Scattered and weak and dying on the ground.
I will be an evergreen not high on a mountain,
    But nestled in a valley by a stream,
        Playing with children,
        Flying kites from my branches,
        Loving the birds that rest there,
        Laughing in the sunshine,
           weeping softly in the rain,

Letting go of all I ever aspired to be,
    For I am already loved,
And that alone is beyond all illusion.

I Did Not Know

I did not know such love existed,
Gentle and fragrant beyond all words,
A dream I never hoped to realize,
Where souls speak and performances end.
God sent you into my life when all my patterns
        of blindness and need had been established,
When I walked the same road again and again
        for love I never got,
When I chose some pseudo-strength that ultimately
        sought to control me and destroy my freedom,
When security became more important
        than life and love!
We were orphans together grown secretly strong,
        both abandoned by cruel manipulation,
Not really able to believe that we had found
        each other.
I thought life had no meaning, that there was only
        endless emptiness,
And I distrusted all that was feminine and strong.
All I know is that love does exist,
That a day and night with you
        are worth all the pain,
And that the love that began so shyly,
        so cautiously,
Can last forever!

Love Breaks Through

When it is time,
    Love breaks through
Like a fragile sprout of Spring,
    softly green and tender,
Crawling sinuously from the dark tomb of earth,
Where first it died only to rise and live.
It appears almost suddenly,
    When it is not watched
And takes its place quietly
    Amid the assorted flowers and trees
        and miracles of life.
At such a moment, the lonely seedpod is forgotten
    And the damp, cold earth of dark incubation
Is but a vague and distant memory.
Love has arrived! Like Spring itself,
    Fragile, but rooted in destiny,
    Newly awakened from sleep
And ready to enjoy the cyclic rhythm
    of each passing year.
To grow and flower, to rest and rise
As was destined when an unseen and loving hand
    First drew life from the chaotic heavens
And foresaw our special, springtime love.

One Day

One day, when stars had disappeared and
    mountains were no longer my friends,
When my favorite river was grey and insensitive
    even to spring's bursting melodies and the
        eloquent Nevada sky said nothing,
When I had lost interest in birds and even trees,
    and the moon upon the giant lake was pale
        and disinterested in earth,
When life had lost flavor and death
    was an unknown terror,
        I was buried in the muck of
          my own despairing.
All former joys were silent, friends had disappeared,
    hope seemed pointless and a dispassionate God
        ignored my imploring,
And there was no one to turn to
    save the poverty I had become,
When my heart begged to break and my eyes
    were glazed with crusty tears
        and I could endure the pain no longer,
I fell upon the ground unable to walk or even crawl,
    admitting life had won and I was alone
        attempting to stand upright on the earth,
That no one could understand the terror
    and loss of confidence I felt,
When love and sex and even gentle touching
    were denied me, and all the gifts I once used
    so facilely were transformed to ineloquent
        stone and stubbornly refused me,

When there was no apparent reason to live
    except I feared the emptiness of death,
I knew that a single yearning appetite could rouse me
    to the beginning of some personal,
        remote salvation,
A single passion, though feeble, could provide
    the light and energy of reconciliation with myself.
And from deep within some cavern of my soul
    heretofore unexplored,
A single word erupted and echoed like a pebble
    rolling down a mountain and said:
"Endure! Endure! The rhythm will return in its
    own time if you do not violate
        some code of honesty with yourself.
"Flowers will reappear, music will return
    to restore your soul!"
Thus slowly I rose from the bottom of the pit
    when every fibre of my being screamed
        for me to lie there still.
I rose up, only to endure, and in the morning
    —for an instant—again saw the sun,
        and rejoiced for the briefest instant
            that I was still alive.
It was then I knew that I would indeed endure,
    and the ever-present pain of some purging
        would finally disappear,
And joy would be forever mine
    in my lonely and redemptive enduring!

To My Friend at 70

Where the hell did the years go? You're still young
    you know!
Wiser, scarred, wounded, but never more alive.
There were times, now almost forgotten, when you
    were
Old before your time—walking, but never
        docilely,
        Towards death,
Sometimes wondering what in the world it was all
    about,
But stubborn enough to stick around and find out,
And too damn stubborn to leave those you love
    or anyone else.
But you're younger now, still so much to learn,
    so much love
        To give and get, so damn much to do
            to make the world warm and liveable
                for all of us,
And now loving and learning and living
    so gratefully.
Hell, 70's not old, giving up is old and
    imprisonment.
Hell, 70's not old, greed is and you've been
    generous all your life
Hell, 70's not old, fear is old and sadness.
    Arrogance is and judgment,
Hell, 70's not old, only life without laughter and
    friends.

Freedom is young, and passion,
　　creativity is young,
　　And excitement, your smile is young and
　　　　eternal hope.
In reality, you've never been younger in your life.
　　So welcome to 70 my friend!

There Were Days

There were days when I wanted the world to know
    that I was alive,
As important as men of power and letters,
As significant a cultural force as names
    in distant textbooks.
I wanted acknowledgement and homage,
    respect and applause.
Now I only want to wake up and see the sky,
    To know that I walk the world joyfully
        like the simple ones of earth.
I want smiles and laughter, flowers
        and a silent meditation by the sea.
I want friends who love me as I am,
    with all my fears and faults,
Who love my very being and presence
    were I never to write a word,
Or achieve anything beyond enjoying the sun
    and the face of a child.
    If life is not serenity, it is nothing,
    If life is not peace, it is warfare.
I have had enough war, enough strife,
    now I look for
    Simplicity and friendship and quiet times,
Satisfied that my power is in the God
    Who lives in my soul
    And directs me as He will,

Until I love only what He wants
    and live as He has destined
Me to live.

Policemen at the Bus Station

Policemen at the bus station, three of them
    trampling a young transient,
Sifting through his wallet like cockroaches
    in a dresser drawer,
His loves and memories strewn about and stained
    by skeletal hands of iron and lead
        and all that's dead and ugly.
Why not rip away his pants
    and check his underwear?
    Did he shower today, wash his hair,
        salute the flag, and brag about the millions
        he saved in taxes?
Transient man-boy with backpack and gentle eyes,
    Your wondering and wandering
        and gentle recollections,
Your loneliness and fear and walking
    through the world alone
    Without a long-haired lady
        or a dog to love you.
I apologize for my race—some call it human—
I apologize
    For the disgrace that law has become
        to all the weak and wounded of the earth.

And as I watch your desecration,
    I want to give you my wallet,
    My strength, my rights to fight
        these uniformed urns of emptiness
        Who love to hassle those who have
            sense enough
    To drift and ponder and question darkness
        and distant stars.
    Your patched beauty more resonant
        than tailored arrogance
        Clutching guns like writhing snakes,
        Challenging you with lizard tongues
        And the decaying voice of legal excrement.
How I despise these probably decent men,
    gathered like snarling dogs
    To tear apart a rabbit—too warm
    and innocent-eyed to live.
I will challenge them, be your attorney,
    your friend, pose as your brother
    If such will save you
        from the degradation
That makes me hate my state, my nation
    and all the rotten legalists
    Who make of law a fence to protect
        their own angry chickens
            And make of freedom a mockery.
Please see my eyes and know I love you
    and your gentleness as much
    As I despise their violence,

Know that the cuffs they jerk roughly on
    are the chains of cowardice
        and a paranoid world slowly disappearing.
You are the future, not they!
    Your questions have currency,
    not their answers!
You are the flower, the distant bell,
    You are the child of heaven,
Brutality and cowardice the voice of hell.

The Script

We followed the script carefully
    through life
    Childhood dreams and football teams
    Walks in the woods
    And love on hay wagons.
We move through college and professions
    Abrupt detours and humble confessions.
    Marriage and kids
    Even divorce and the pain
        that wouldn't go away.
We changed jobs,
    dreamed of mounting investments
    And every possible success,
    Chased hobbies and rainbows
    Made love and knew that it would
        all go on forever.
Each page of the script was numbered,
    few mysteries or difficult words,
Hurts enough and bleeding,
    but we hurried on, ignored the wounds
        and they went away.
Something always worked to hold us together.

Then one day, silently, suddenly,
  it all came apart,
And we turned the page and discovered
Nothing else had been written.
We were alone with blank pages,
  with our confusion and fear,
    With fleeting time and words
That had to be written privately, uniquely
    in the depths of our own hearts,
Without any script but our own!

The Laughers

Well, the homeless wanderers are laughing
    at the pinstripe boys
    Who struggle for their six-figure income,
And the pinstripers smile patronizingly
    at the vagabonds
    Who carry their meager life's fortunes
        in a backpack.
The career women laugh at housewives
    who are slaves
    To the kitchen and the Junior League,
And the housewives laugh at the career women
    who are slaves
    To the loneliness of the climb
        up the corporate mountain.
The young laugh at the old who would rather talk
    and sip wine than frolic on skateboards.
And the old laugh at the young
    who don't know what lies ahead.
The police laugh at the hippies,
    the hippies mock the police,
The banker laughs at the repossessed and the
    repossessed finally laugh at the banker
        when they remember the lilies of the field
And the Son of man who had no place whereon
    to rest his head.
Lawyers laugh at the bullies and cowards who hide
    behind lawyers and almost everyone
        laughs at lawyers.

The environmentalist laughs bitterly
     at the stumbling governments
          and artists laugh at the greedy developers.
But only wise and gentle ones have courage
     to laugh at themselves and all of life's madness,
To recognize finally and securely
     that any life is a prison,
          in America or Moscow, South Africa,
               India, or Poughkeepsie,
Until we know that the freedom to be one's true
     and inner self
Is the only lasting and imperishable wealth.

Kidnapped

I was a kidnapped child, stolen
    from his own backyard,
    Transported to sudden manhood
Before his tears had dried.

I was an abused child, beaten
    by no one but virtue,
    Tied to another's traditions
And forbidden to interrogate the clouds.

I was an autistic child, speaking
    only what others taught,
    Communicating in silence to the trees
In a language no one ever seemed to hear.

I was a retarded child, smiling softly
    to keep the curious away,
    Afraid to ask questions,
Only because no one ever answered them.

Finally the years have passed,
    but scars and memories endure,
    And I can rejoice in privacy to be
The shy, loving child I always was.

People Gather

The people gather in the corridors
    of the courts
Children confused
    and parents relieved and angry
Dreams that died and new hopes
    budding tenderly—
Love transformed to anger,
    children the unwitting victims
Likely to repeat the same mistakes
And return to the same courts
With the same failures and abandoned hopes.
So much anger looking for love
    In some distant relationship
Or some unfounded illusion
As if love is not available
    to us all within the boundaries
        of our own hearts.
But here is a segment of life in the raw
Not as *Cosmopolitan* writes,
    but as survival dictates.
So much patience is needed,
    so much love possible
        when anyone can see and understand.
Not all appear in the courts
    to discolor and abandon
        what has been gathered through the years
Some are content to conceal what has happened
    and to live together
        the life of silence and separation.

But in the courts, the people gather—
    waiting to fight for what is theirs—
Tragedy beyond television,
    victories and failures beyond Broadway plays—
Life as it is, not as we choose and select,
As the people gather in the corridors of the courts!

Studying My Anxieties

Studying my anxieties,
Stretching out across my complex world
    Like telephone wires still in contact
With unnumbered, unnamed fears
    offering no salvation.
They must be ignored or confronted,
    as I fly above and beyond them,
    My feet winged with some new desire.
Enough time pacing the floor,
Enough time keeping score
    Of ancient fears and disappointments.
Life is now, even now, always now!
Enough reflection that only uncovers
    What had to be covered.
The old way worked long enough,
    My hopes were always hopeful enough.
Now vainly I try to become again
    What I once was, but the way is barred.
And I move on hopefully, courageously,
    To a new serenity and peace,
Ignoring my anxieties.

Danny Was Talking

Danny was talking about the time
    when a special lady used
    To invite him over for a home-cooked meal,
But it sure as hell doesn't happen anymore.
    Beverly spends an hour getting ready
        for a movie
And seems convinced that just the right shade
    of eye shadow
    And maybe a generous hint
        of in-depth cleavage
Will turn Danny's heart to warm raspberry jelly.
    So they go to the movies, then out for dinner,
And eat exotic things like smoked salmon
    and escargots
    When a few months ago
        she didn't seem to know
Oysters Rockefeller from broiled sand dabs.
    After dinner, she disappears
        to rearrange her eye shadow,
And maybe to readjust the in-depth cleavage as well,
        And Danny goes home wondering
        if women's liberation
Has put out the word against home-cooked meals.
    One thing for sure,
        as far as Danny is concerned,
All the eye shadow and cleavage in the world
    Are a hundred miles farther away from marriage

Than kisses and conversation in the kitchen,
And a simple, loving, home-cooked meal.

When the Therapist

When the therapist told me it was my overbearing
    mother and insensitive father, an arrogant
        Church and a starved culture
That made me the wreck I was,
    I had a few gentle questions.
    Who gave me my smile, my love of trees
        and mountains,
    My yearning to be a friend,
        a heart filled with love,
    And even a tormented brain
        forever on the verge of laughter?
Was it the same mother and father,
    the same Church and starved culture?
I also wondered if I could meet the therapist's parents
    and find out what kind of kid he was?
Could we share photo albums, old high school
    yearbooks, swap lovers for a night,
        spend a weekend camping or riding
        a raft down a white-
        water river?
Could we snowshoe through the Sierra,
    trudge across the desert,
Have a lemon pie contest to see whose meringue
    came out intact?

Could we spend a day with my mother, read
    poetry, visit my old school and blow an
        afternoon with my dog?
Maybe we could plant tomatoes together,
    bullshit at a lonely bar in Yuma, ski cautiously
        around moguls, turn an edge
            and roll helplessly on our asses?
Could we to to the circus, pick up ladies
    at a Caribbean resort,
Play Trivial Pursuits, have a pillow fight,
    Indian wrestle, meditate and tell jokes
        after too much beer?
And finally we could bury all judgments
    on mothers and fathers, churches and cultures,
        and accept responsibility for ourselves.
Then we could sit still together and wonder
    if we'd ever have to therapize again.

Most

Most are content to let their dreams die,
Not the superficial ones of money and success,
Recognition and sex beyond description,
But the soul dreams that could change a lonely,
    wounded world.
What courage it takes to cling to a dream
    in the face of abandonment!
Ultimately it will destroy you
    in the most total loneliness of all.
A rare love can intervene and open doors
    that have been sealed by steel
        and centuries.
Now I do not look at a woman
    with the lust of adolescence,
Or the beauty that culture recognizes as profound.
I only see her aura of kindness and warmth,
    honesty and compassion.
She can fathom a dream
    no matter how distant and difficult.
Her makeup and hairstyle,
    so inconsequential to me
        absorbs more time than the tuning of her soul.
    Does no one know that death comes
    and takes all the eye shadow away,
Leaving only a spirit honed or neglected.
Apparently loving couples, laughing, rushing,
    gathering, travelling,
        Are the very killers of dreams.

Strangers to each other at any level
 but the apparent surface,
And content with clichés no matter how varied,
 intellectual or clever.
The soul mate I seek probably lives in a cave
 and I will never find her—
Though I notice I pay more attention
 to caves the last few years than anything else!

Every Fear

Every fear in the world conspired against me
    when seemingly for decades
        I was never afraid.
I left you, only to return when illusions reappeared
    and you received me with love—
Till finally even your love grew frightened,
        but never faint
And you feared that my desperate hunger
    for some illusive satisfaction
Would destroy you as well as
    some abandoned child.
Only when you were no longer available
Did I return to the core of my soul
    And recognize the love I had lost.
Perhaps I came in desperation, but it seemed more
    in a painful realization that time moved
        and each day was but its own emptiness.
I who had wanted the stars wanted only your arms
    and would trade every victory
        for your heart and soul
            enwrapped in mine.
I was a warrior in my way,
    mortally wounded a hundred times,
        refusing love's surgery and healing.

Love had been acclaim from afar at talent and
    strength.
    I never believed you could love my weakness
        as well and
    assuage the savage, indescribable hurt
    unattended from childhood.
The battle is not won, but it is begun—on a real
    field with real soldiers—
        not in the fog of my own consciousness.
Tonight as you lie in my arms, I know I am loved
    and tomorrow I will more fearlessly take each
        child's step that leads to happiness.

I Looked Up

I looked up and there you were,
All my dreams and some I never dreamed,
Standing on what appeared to be two good-sized
    feet.
Hell, I never got beyond your face,
The smile that jumped from your lips and landed
        in your
The whole sudden experience took me by surprise,
And I felt the fear pulling at my chest, insisting
        That you could never love me.
I wanted to push it all aside for once in my life,
Jump across the room and take chances
        I never took before.
I wanted to tell you all the things you wouldn't like
        Before you had a chance
           to find out for yourself:
To tell you of a boy who only looks like a man,
Of an unshed tear that only looks like a smile,
Of courage that only stands strong
        with trembling knees,
Of rough hands that finally can only be gentle,
And of a lover who only whispers because
        You are too beautiful to talk to.
A thousand men in every town and language want
    you.
How the hell could you ever want me?

Life Has Its Beginnings

Life has its beginnings,
    Each with its own
Special promises,
    Each a door opening
To some new wonder,

Each a unique melody fashioned
    in our hearts,
Each a personal adventure
    even as at time's beginning
When darkness was dispelled
    and the sun and moon
Were first appointed to guard
    the heavens and lovingly
To guide the day and night.

Such beginnings are a renewal
    of our very being,
A sometimes fragile gift
    That must be tended and loved,
    Nourished and understood,
Until all that can be, will be,
And life continues to be
    a joyful creation
Of promises and original melodies
    and endless new beginnings.

Everyone Wonders

Everyone wonders what a grown man like Harry's
    doing
    Whispering his love-words to a teenager
Who blushes at everything he says and wants to
    live with him forever.
The psychologists understand: she is only a child
    looking for the father she never had.
Obviously! And Harry is clutching desperately
    his lost youth.
But what of the wife who long ago wanted
    to murder him?
Is she merely longing to eviscerate the father
    who eviscerated her?
Is she a more deserving target
    of Harry's love words?
    With her cynical wisdom
        and snarling comprehension of the way it is?
Or does Harry merely seek novelty
    when sags and stretch marks
        tarnish his illusion?
It is the stretch marks of the soul that put him off.
Harry has had pain enough and refuses
    to be a receptacle of hers.
Let the critics join Freud and Jung at bridge.
    Harry feels good,
    His dreams are again intact.
So he whispers his love-words to a teenager
    Who blushes at everything he says,
And wants to live with him forever.

Those Times

In those times of pain and sadness
That float in like a silent fog,
    Everyone has an answer for me,
        Well meaning and certainly effective,
From jogging and self-denial, less sleep
    and more time
        To smell the flowers
            until my sinuses ache.
Strange, when all is moving well and rhythmically,
    I don't need any help, and when it isn't,
        Nothing ever seems to work.
Perhaps there is nothing anyone can do for me
    save me,
    And I can only do it by not doing it.
I will float with life, surrender to its anger
    and sadness,
    Await its joy and wonder and hope
    that the God
        Who seems to somehow guide my life,
Will not leave me too long alone
    in the painful darkness.

Weary of Wrestling

I am weary of wrestling with the day
    And making the night prisoner,
Ignoring the simple beauty as one gone blind,
    lost in the endless crevices of my own mind.
I want the wind to pass through my body
    as it does the air,
I want the earth to wrap my roots as a flower
And the clouds to descend upon my brain
And lift me to the heavens like an idle hawk
    soaring in the wind.
I have lived long enough to prove nothing anymore,
To let love have its day and faith direct my way
Like the music of violins singing
    from an unseen hilltop.
I want all life's energies to circle through my being
    like a ring of cleansing breath
That laughs at disappointments and makes
    a mockery of death.

The Days Drift By

The days drift by without names or numbers
    And I watch and wonder if they will ever be as
        they were.
Childhood cannot be over, the laughs that rang
    through the neighborhood
    I want to find in your eyes.
Lead me from this pit of pain
    where darkness looms,
    So that I can again make your face
    glow with laughter.
Some pain is locked inside,
    defying key or combination, eluding
    The finest chemistry
        and the most skillful knife.
I do not ask much of life
    Pizza and cold beer after tennis
    A quiet walk along the back roads
    Some serenity I could always feel
        gazing at the trees.
Who came and stole away my joy?
Who told me that life got easier?
Who taught me how to live too late?
I would like to look down the road a year or two
    and see how I am.
Meanwhile I hang on, believing, hoping,
    somehow knowing
    That I have been knocked from my horse,
    Blinded by a too-bright light
That soon enough will direct me
    to life and love again.

Calling Banks

Calling banks these days to check the pulse of my
    mortgage
Or anything more complicated than the rates of T-
    bills,
    Is like trying to get your brother-in-law out of
    the Kremlin
        On a weekend pass.
Since I have a fresh mortgage with the
    Westamerica Bank,
    Which sounds as mellifluous as the Mayflower,
I wanted to know why they charged me three
    points over prime when I had been promised
    two.
But since all the operators were busy ("sorry about
    that")
I waited patiently for Maureen who gave me an
    800 number
    And a long explanation of why the
    Westamerica Bank had sold my mortage to
    someone she didn't know
    And why she knew neither the amount or the
    interest rate, but only my monthly payment.
Assuredly the 800 number would know except that
    a recorded operator
    Informed me I was in an area not covered by
    the 800 number.
I called Maureen back, waited for an endless,
    "Sorry about that!"
    And finally got Linda (Maureen went home

sick, revealing wondrous judgment) who kept
me waiting long enough
To write this poem and two others,
Only to be lectured that not all 800 numbers were
valid everywhere,
Until it seemed my fault for believing Maureen
in the first place.
Now you may understand why I am gradually
getting rid of all
Mortgages, banks, Lindas, faceless mortgage
companies,
Not to mention sick Maureens and all 800
numbers,
And emulating crazy old Uncle Al who kept his
money in coffee cans
And paid cash for everything.
He sure was crazy, smiling all day long,
Travelling the whole world, loving everyone,
Eating everything, and convinced until he died
at ninety-seven
That IRS was a little-known British branch of the
IRA.

You're the Kind of Person

You're the kind of person who could have been
    anything you wanted to be.
You're also the kind of person who doesn't give a
    damn about money, fame, reputation,
    government,
        religious wars, South American coups,
    inflation, unemployment,
        or the effect of the killer bee on the
    national economy.
What the hell's wrong with you?

Do Not Tame Me

Do not tame me and bind me
    And whisper your litany of fears I do not
        share.
Do not capture me and cage me in the prison
    of my own doubts.
Do not crush me with tears and threats
    and angry screams of my sacred duties.
I have been dutiful enough, docile enough, kind
    enough to be dull and restless.
I was born with a Viking's blood
    and Beowulf's heart,
With Charlemagne's vision and Roland's trumpet.
The man-boy who seems older now still wants
    to play with the world,
To tease rivers and walk above cities,
To reveal the secrets of human hearts
    And to bring hope to those
        who have lost their way.
I want a love that tears me in half with caring,
A passion that leaps beyond cautious friendship,
A joy that makes the gods envious
    and the giants at the center of the earth
        inflamed with jealousy.
But do not tame me and hold me
    and whisper your litany of fears
    And tell me you love the passionless man
        I have become.

Gentle Old Woman

Gentle old woman with her shopping bag
Shuffling through Kresge's to find a little yarn
    —just the right shade of purple—
To hold her flowered hat in an unfriendly wind.
"I almost lost it twice," she tells me,
"And I thought it was a goner under the
    Greyhound bus."
Fragile as a desert's fast-departing flower
Wrinkled with memories and spotted like a child
    freckled in the sun
Chuckling softly at her own feebleness,
Finally satisfied with the delicate purple of a
    Jacaranda tree
"Not too tight," she tells me,
"No sense croaking before my time"
Hat in place, crowned with faded flowers,
She extracts three pennies from deep within her
    beaded purse, still determined to pay her way.
I hold the heavy door,
And watch her shuffle, still chuckling
    into the wind,
Climbing her own Everest,
Winning her own Olympics,
Solving the day's problem with just the
    right shade of purple.

Strangers

I sat in a crowded, smoke-filled room of strangers,
And listened to their testimonies of wounds
    never healed
    Beautiful women who forever feel ugly
    Strong men who feared a supermarket
        or driving on a freeway.
There is so much we don't know as analysts guess
    and doctors ponder.
How long does it take to listen to God's voice
    within our own soul,
The only voice of truth and freedom?
When is it quiet enough to hear?
Who is strong enough to drown the shouts of all
    who would make us in their own image and
        likeness?
As has been said, "Pain is a cruel doctor,
    but he is the only one we really listen to."
And none of us in the room would ever again be
    strangers!

I Left Love

I left love lingering on a hundred doorsteps,
Feared lest the door would close
    And I would be more desolate than before.
Is there time for a man whose whole being pulses
    to love?
    To find a soul as lost and longing,
    As full and resonant as my own?
Is there place in a world I do not comprehend?
    I only live to love, there is nothing left for me.
All that I have accomplished pales
    Before a single kiss of soul to soul,
And for that I will give my life
    Without recompense or regret.

When I'm Normal

Will you love me when I'm normal,
When I don't wake you in the middle
    of the night
And wonder if I'll ever write again?
When I don't whisper to you in
    a romantic scene in a movie
And wonder if the scars of divorce
    and attorneys will ever go away?
Past guilts and future calamities?
When I ignore the patter of rain
    and the rush of wind at night
And wonder if a bleeding gum
    means I'll lose my teeth.
What if I don't worry about last night's dream
    when snakes cornered me on an anthill,
Or if I wake up wondering if we
    shouldn't refinance the house or
    drive the jeep off a cliff to collect
    on insurance,
        And repeat the same fears I've been
            boring you with for the last two weeks?
What if I don't worry about burnout,
    About computers making everyone over 30
        obsolete,
Or if I miss my three-mile morning
    walk and wonder if I'm over the hill,
Or notice that my backhand in tennis has
    lost its zip.

Or change my mind three times in an hour,
    postpone two vacations and plan three more?

Will you still love me when I'm normal
    And don't think I should be a
        mortgage broker or a carpet salesman
        for a while,
When I forget your aunt's name and
    wonder if I'm an early case of Alzheimer's,
When you forget the cream in my coffee
    And I wonder who you've been having coffee
        with,
When I wonder if we shouldn't move to
    Ireland where writers don't pay taxes,
When I ask you seven times if the plot
    of a new story sounds okay,
Or read a poem three times to make sure
    you really love it?
When I wonder if I'm useful for
    anything but bringing warmth to a
        living room chair,
When I'm sure I'm past my prime
    And falling apart because I don't
        know the names of the three top musical
        groups?

What if I just worry about the IRS,
    the weather, poor garbage service,
    and my right-rear tire, and losing
    things on my computer—not to mention
    keys, glasses, my wallet, and the
        only pair of socks I like with my brown
           suit?
Do you think—when I'm normal—
    you'll still love me?

It's Eye-Catching Time

It's eye-catching time,
The eloquent language of the city
    More honest than most of its words.
I want you
    But if I told you
    You'd probably run away.
So I'll just look
    On streets and subways
    Through car windows
    In supermarkets
    And restaurants
And maybe I'll catch your eye
    And wonder.

Love Alone Heals

Love alone heals
    The torn ligaments of a lifetime
    The limping, wounded, shredded legs
        that tried in vain
    To climb a mountain finally too tall!
Love alone heals
    The broken bones and battered limbs of living
    The weary, bleeding, aching arms
        that cling in vain
    To trees in hurricane and conquering winds.
Love alone heals
    The congealed sadness and hidden fears
    The buried madness and unshed tears
        that hoped in vain
    To still the roar of endless oceans.
Love alone heals
    The hearts that knocked at empty doors
    And crawled across the splintered floors
        to search in vain
    For soothing breezes in a fragrant valley.
Love alone heals
    And waits in silence for the storms to cease
    Offering only laughter and unshaken peace
        for those who tried in vain
    To find their frantic, tearful way alone
    And finally found it—waiting patiently at
        home.

I Have Walked

I have walked in lands where there are no paths
    or footprints,
No guided tours or warnings posted
    for the unsuspecting,
Where visas are denied and passports
    have no validity.
    Lands frozen with monsters of childhood
        and strange museums of assorted horrors.
    Lands of flowers with dark, staring eyes,
        and trees with gaunt, grasping fingers,
    Sullen lands where silence lives and ancient fears
        blow from nowhere like the wind,
Where men and women stand alone
    amid darkness and sinister visions
        beyond all retelling.
I go there when someone demands it, despite tears
    and fears that I cannot survive another visit.
I return when an unseen hand mercifully opens
    a healing door and plead like a child
        in the hope I have finally escaped.
But perhaps I must go there again and again
    until I am brave enough to bring
        light to the flowers' eyes and warmly shake
        the hands of the frightening trees.
Thus to create light in darkness, as a true child of
    God with power and courage
        granted only to those few
Who are admitted to the lands
    without paths or footprints
    And love finally confronts loneliness
        at its core.

All These Years

It took me all these years to lay a foundation,
To find mortar and bricks, level land and an acre
    all my own.
Now I will place each pillar of support cautiously
    and firmly,
Simplify my elaborate architectural plans,
Content with a single room, securely roofed, that
    is warm and friendly and mine.
Now I am no longer who I thought I was,
    Designer of palaces and mansions,
Master of light and power and rising towers
    of affluence and success.
I am only what I always was, a kid from Kalamazoo
    who sold magazines and peddled papers,
        mowed grass and transplanted bushes
Chopped down weeds and watered flowers.
But I will have my house, smaller than I imagined,
But finally all mine, where I can hide and emerge,
    laugh and reflect and light soft, flickering candles
        as beautiful as any
    Cathedral or elaborate estate.
There are music and books, food and warmth and
    light, and a friend or two who grin at my
        jokes and look at me with
    love and respect beyond any possibility of loss
    or remission.
They know and I know—and it does not matter if
    it took all these years to lay a foundation.

Who Says?

Who says "You can't go home,"
When there's no place else to go,
And fear crowds in uninvited to reduce me
    to a helpless child?
I am looking for a mother, lover, a friend
    and companion,
Someone to take my hand and walk with me
    through dark hallways
    And mornings when there is no sun.
I am weary of struggling alone,
    of denying my pain
    With triumphs and smiles and memories.
I have done the best I can, sought solace in a
    hundred hopes,
That finally proved more hopeless
    than healing balm
    To a confused mind and anxious heart.
Each day I surrender to a God I cannot see or hear,
Each hour I submit to His will and ask only
    Enough light to take the next faltering step.
I want to go home where love waits for no reason
    at all,
Where beauty and laughter abide as the only
    antidote
    To death and despair.
I have heard a thousand times that I must grow
    up,
    Walk whole and self-sufficient under my own
        power,

Believe in myself, love myself, and understand
    I am God's child.
Now I only want to go home and surrender to my
    own helplessness,
    Because there's no place else to go.

Life Has Become a Tightrope

Life has become a tightrope
    Where I walk too carefully
Balancing myself against each contusion,
Steadying myself against all confusion,
Arming myself with any suitable illusion,
    Cautiously, carefully making my way
        to the other side,
Then turning around and trying it again.

Esau's

Well, the coffee's good at Esau's and the sausage
    tastes homemade,
But the early morning conversation wouldn't make
    the president very happy
When the street people, crawling from benches and
    beaches and deserted doorways in Santa
    Barbara,
Assemble quietly to face another day amid wealth
    and tranquillity.
Johnny tells me about his epilepsy and the half-
    truths in the paper,
Still wonders why Kennedy had to die when he
    gave the country a chance.
Johnny used to sleep at the Salvation Army for five
    bucks a night,
    But he finally extended his leave
        and can't come back anymore.
He's afraid of a seizure on the beach, remembering
    the last time
    When they took his prized watch
        and even his backpack.
        "They left me my shorts," he laughs,
        "But the country
        "Don't seem to have a heart anymore.
        "Nobody cares very much like they used
        to.
        "It was my own kind that took my
        backpack . . ."
Johnny sips his coffee because the "damn

dilantin"
Won't let him eat until eleven o'clock and
makes his head all jumbled
　　with crazy thoughts.
Where will he go today? Move a few chairs, maybe
　　a piano,
　　Clean a damp basement or shovel leaves and
　　　　dog shit for the rich.
Soft-spoken and blonde, nice looking and clean,
　　laughs easily,
　　No time to worry about his identity or what it
　　　　all means.
Maybe it's better when you got nothing except
　　today,
　　Like "the birds of the air and the lilies of the
　　　　field"
And all those peaceful things Christ used to talk
　　about
　　Before the Christians turned them into more
　　　　palatable words,
Like "redemption" and "salvation" and the
　　building fund.

I Would Create

I would create a refuge for the lonely ones,
The brave sensitive, ravaged spirits who travel
    forever alone,
The assemblage of the wounded who appear
    on city streets at night
        Like dwarfed and disfigured members
            of another race.
We who have lost our way, wonder profoundly
    if solace and comfort exist,
        Struggle to make each day mean something,
Find no one to love who does not want to make us
    a prisoner.
For us the family is no suitable symbol,
Because we are the orphans separated and
    unwanted as we are.
Must we die in routine and a love parceled out
    like a reward
        For good behavior?
We are the victims of the strong and self-assured,
    ready to grasp
        Any hand that will lead us from terror.
We live with endless fantasies and illusions,
Have no time to lay foundations and build love.
The marriages we see do not thrill us,
Friendship alone seems to endure and rejuvenate.
Is there a key to the labyrinth that only the
    privileged
        Deserve to find?

The rest must struggle with madness and
    emptiness and fear.
My mission is to them, and I would create a refuge
    To give the lonely ones like me
        hope and love.

At Times

At times the mountains seem insurmountable now
As I gaze at them from the safety of a warm,
    flowering meadow
There is snow upon the peaks and chill winds
    gust angrily above me.
Yet, as beautiful as the meadow is, I have been
    here too long
And the song of birds has grown dull,
The flowers seem artificial, and the frogs
    too content.
I want to fly myself above the peaks, sing
    my own songs,
And climb till every vestige of every dream
    is silent
Why am I afraid to travel where destiny draws me?
Why do I hesitate when a familiar echo deep
    in the caverns of my heart calls me?
This is no time to reminisce, to watch
    the circling crows and drifting clouds.
It is time to move lest winter harden my limbs
    and freeze my fantasies.
It is time to move boldly and bravely and remember
That the purest air is waiting in the heights
And a single step is enough to be on my way!

Once I Thought

Once I thought it was my accomplishments
   you loved,
The obvious victories that were apparent
   to everyone who saw
      but the shell and not the man-boy who lived
         within.
Now I know there is some connection of souls,
   some destiny that is beyond all reckoning,
And that the joy of a sunrise is more valuable than
   all the neon.
As I gaze out the winter window and see the grey-
   green grass spattered with brown,
The bare trees, lonely distant mountains,
   and grey skies,
I realize how little in my life has changed.
No one taught me of love except by loving me—
   unconditionally—
Standing forever at my side when there was every
   human reason to abandon me.
Shortcuts are no longer available, my whole being
   centers within, and the power of God is mine
Only because I am His child, His expression,
   His manifestation of love, valuable only
      as I know I am.
Now I know there is nothing that can harm me
   if I but cling to Him,
And see each season of pain and confusion
   as His loving effort to restore me

To what was always there in childhood, in
     manhood, in the expression of gratitude that I
     am loved no matter what, no matter how,
Only because I am.

Déjà Vu

So much *déjà vu*
>Of politicians' promises and rich men's
>>ambitions,
>Of dull day succeeding dull day,
>Of yesterday's newspaper quarreling
>>with tomorrow's,
>>>Over star wars and oil prices,
>>>Over prayer in school and mediocre
>>>>teachers,
>>>Over death in St. Louis and rape in
Texas,
>>>Over wholesale prices and economic
>>>>terrors,
>>>Over lotteries and cancer and new-
model cars.
So much *déjà vu* of bright young men and beautiful
>women,
Of octogenarians and premature deaths,
Of football and baseball and cocaine,
Of all the winners and losers in assorted games.
Who will make the news today? The best dressed,
The worst treated, the underfed and overheated?
>>And I will walk gently under the stars
>>Studying the sky and knowing that I am
>>>myself *deja vu*,
If I live another hour without you.

I Love You

After all the years of running and climbing
    mountains,
I have finally longed for my home—
    weary of being alone—
    Tired of living by myself
    Sated with strangers who only share
        the stories shared with anyone
            who will listen—
For years triumphs were enough, but they
    did not consider my heart
Which needed to give and receive
    that which was reserved solely for you.
It was only when I wanted to die,
    When the path I chose seemed already too
        familiar.
There is another mountain to climb,
    quiet nights by the fire, courage to face
    the fears that I avoided all my life,
And I want you at my side when my
    pseudo-strength deserts me, and to be
        there for you as well.
I cannot forever promise you more than I am,
But I will be here with all I have to give,
    Weary of illusions
    Tired of fantasies
    Sated with vain imaginings that ask nothing
        and give little as well.
Each day I will try to confront what I avoided,
To face life as it is and not as I want it to be

You have loved me so long and the pain in my
    heart longs to let go and love you in return.
Somehow your courage and endurance taught me
    more of life than all the rest and
I wish I could remain to learn what all the
    wandering never taught me.

Cozy and Familiar

I would like a small house on a busy street,
    cozy and familiar,
Friends around the corner and satisfaction in
    whatever I do.
My own values are simple enough
    and I am filled with light that quarrels with
      the darkness.
I will have it all, the simplicity and the joy
    and the courage to bring it about,
Not like some giant, vigorous entrepreneur,
But a quiet man who finally knows that all life
    is in reality at the center of his own being.
All my defenses are torn down, my face hides
    nothing anymore,
    my heart beats every note it feels.
There must be a reason for all of this,
    God's reason,
      so I ask no more questions and live my life
      as I can
Longing for simplicity, quiet joy, and
    a small house on a busy street,
      cozy and familiar.

Charlie

I used to think that age would bring you
    Maturity and mellowness,
    Wisdom and money,
    Fame, culture, and contentment,
  Even an honorable mention for the Nobel Prize,
  Or at least some suitable, syrupy civic award.
But I now know that you'll never change,
    Forever the same
    Stubborn, opinionated,
    Slovenly, cantankerous,
    Pompous, outrageous,
  Loveable bastard you've always been!

What a relief!

Diana

I see your frightened face
And crooked, hysterical smile,
Your deep, sad eyes and your whole body
    thirsting for love.
Even your children appear to pass you by
    with strength and beauty,
    Wisdom and understanding and confidence
That seem to have deserted you.
Your husband builds his empire, then rebuilds it,
    like a child playing with blocks.
And you turn on the projector of your dreams
    playing a different role each day,
Longing for excitement and love, longing for
    fulfillment and digging a tunnel of freedom to
    release the fragments that flow from your
    soul with power and depth.
Each morning you want to run away,
But life is an unfeeling jailer who offers you no
    simple escape.
It seems too late, to write, to sing, to dance,
    to make a parent, perhaps long dead,
        pay attention.
Freedom is now only a word, too costly and
    painful to pursue.
So you dream and wonder and hope,
    And time passes until your heart grows
    narrow enough to stay docile
        within your chest.
And only your frightened eyes and gentle,
    hysterical smile
Reveal what no one but you seems attentive to.

There Are Thousands

There are thousands walking the streets tonight—
Hand in hand laughing and planning vacations in
    the mountains,
Remembering love in the afternoon
    And lingering as if anywhere is everywhere in
      the world.
Why do I walk alone with no one to share some of
    the most vibrant moments of my life?
A man could draw straws and find a lover,
Cling to an empty hand in a crowd,
Grasp eyes on an elevator,
Answer an ad and head for Portugal forever.
Am I nothing without a woman?
I've heard the platitudes and brave psychologists
Who tell me to find it all within myself!
No longer! I have waited too long—
Soon I will give up this vacuous freedom
For a tender, gentle lady as lovely and needy as I—
Someone to walk with along the beach
To talk with at dawn when sleep eludes me,
To make coffee in the morning and tell me a
    hundred times a day—
    with gestures and word and love looks
That I am the dream that came true—
    While thousands—lonely and lost—still walk
    the streets.

Strange

Strange how I forget the anger,
The plots to hold and entrap me,
The curses and litany of deprecations
  Ones I thought I deserved.
Now I only remember the quiet nights by the fire
  watching TV,
Favorite cookies that defied rationing,
And that special way of finally settling
  into cuddling sleep.
After three shifts of position as precise as a drill
  team.
The rage has no meaning or currency, for
  "to understand all is to forgive all" indeed.
Life is strange! Who would live it if we
  could foresee the pain?
Who can live it if the pain is not somehow
  forgotten?
I am grateful for a memory that recalls
  only what was warm and loving,
So that somehow life can begin again
    With love and laughter, and wisdom that
      could never have come any other way,
Grateful for a God who sees only mistakes, not
  crimes,
    and gives us another chance to understand—
      until our final breath.

Too Soon

It was too soon for love
As if we had both lived long enough
    to know that love is patient and gentle,
Beyond narcissism and self-gratification.
It moves now like clouds brushing across the
    moon,
Like a wheat field in a soft breeze
Like the ocean's waves on quiet, balmy night.
We will love soon enough without techniques
    or maneuvers borrowed from the past,
No love on the dotted line for us, no rote
    recitations of passion practiced a hundred
        times before.
We have known the sudden passion of the
    tempestuous years
    with its own special delight,
The abrupt seduction that left us still feeling all
    alone.
I made more love to your fingers than I have
    made in the past in a hundred ravagings.
Our love will come like the soft breeze that teases
    the trees,
Like the cool air of morning that makes us shudder
    with delight.
Now there are two people here—who know how
    much
    love can hurt, who know how long
        childhood wounds
    take to heal, who know that pain is

real enough to kill,
and who finally know—after years of
searching and aching
When it is time for love and not too soon.

When the Western Sky Softens

When the western sky softens and the sun
    dissolves
    in rose and gold splendor,
To announce the end of another day together,
Words elude me and memories take possession
    of my soul.
I wonder where life has directed me,
    If decisions I made a decade ago have made
        me a prisoner of my past,
If there is still time and passion to bring the earth
    alive,
    And to gather flowers along the back roads.
Or if the banalities of responsibility have dulled
    the spark
    That first ignited our love.
And when the sun is finally gone
    And darkness turns the ocean to ink and the
        sky to ebony,
I search for the stars and attend the rhythm
    of the waves.
    Then my heart is briefly at rest, energy fills
        my being,
And I am certain that every ancient dream
    will be realized.

The Warmth

I like the warmth of you
Cuddling against me in the night,
Holding me close against the storms of manhood
And the residue of childish fears.
I lose myself in your softness
And bid the morning to walk softly
    lest it startle me with the remnants of
        disquieting dreams
And when the sun rises and the coffee is brewing
When the fire is roaring and the trees shake off the
    night in a gentle breeze,
I wish there were words to penetrate the barrier
    between us.
But no words come and we talk of what we always
    talk
And smother the silence that leads to truth and
    love.
I have not failed in life
I did the best I could to heal scars and repair
    shattered bones
That were broken before I was strong enough
    to protest.
Yet I still search for that intimate love
Where fantasy is not needed to excite me
And my sex is as normal as my breathing
Still search in my innermost being
For not to know such love is not to have lived.

Surrender

Surrender to what is and love yourself
    in innocence—
Knowing that a benign spirit
    lives within you
And each cycle of life will pass
    as you move forward
To the joy and serenity that were
    always meant to be you!
Live beyond concern and fear,
    knowing that love is stronger than
    any of these imposters.
There is nothing to be afraid of,
Light is at every moment within your rea
    As you grow towards what you
        were eternally meant to be,
            and already are from child

Surrender to what is and love yourself i
    innocence—
The pain will disappear in the light.
And the power that is yours,
    Beyond ambition or false security,
Will fill your being with peace
    That nothing else can give
There is an energy that you
    have never known, that flows
    like the tide and the
        gentle motion of clouds.

You will never again be alone
for the light is your constant companion.
As you surrender to what is
And love yourself in innocence.

Lying Together

Lying together in silence because all the words are
    used up,
Secretly afraid to tell the truth lest I lose my
    artificial limbs,
Hoping to grow strong enough not to compromise
    or be humiliated
    By every organ-grinder with a monkey.
Not quite brave enough to go it alone until all the
    pieces are in place,
Or to endure the silence that echoes so loudly
    on itself.
Patiently waiting for a sign from heaven or hell,
    No longer expecting love but still believing
        it can happen
    At least as often as any other eclipse.
Longing to be revered but caught in a private
    madness that makes it impossible,
Struggling at least to believe in God or the eternity
    of oceans and mountains,
Searching the skies for freedom and whispering
    to the clouds
    Because no one else seems to hear.
Dancing when I want to walk, untouched when I
    want to be embraced,
Afraid to venture forth or explore what claims
    to be mine,
    But guards itself like a private garden, watered
        as well by strangers as by one true love.

Still wondering if love will ever happen, but finally
wise enough
Not to die in the desert when there is a patch
of grass to lie on.
Almost believing that patience conquers
everything, even love,
But knowing that it never happened to father
or brother or friend,
And wondering why I still think it will happen to
me.

Gentleness

I have never know such gentleness as yours before,
    Never knew that love could whisper with such
    quiet reverence.
If there is a God Who cares for man,
    He will give me time before I die
        To absorb the gentleness
            that pours from your very skin.
Your courage frightens me, encourages me.
I am now such fragility
    When once I was only strength.
But then you would not have loved me,
    Nor would I have seen your soul.
Only in weariness and desperation could I have felt
    your love,
    And known a gentleness I have never known
        before.

Loving You

Loving you blends with all the sights and
    sounds of an ocean night
The sighing and washing of the waves
    Rhythmically rolling the velvet sand
    in a thousand sensuous forms.
The distant moaning of the seals
    slithering and fondling in a hidden cove,
The pleading music of crickets in the slopes above
The silver reflection of the moon
    dancing on the eyes of the dark water
The soft shadows moving stealthily
    across the mounds of sand and rocks
The moist, shimmering seaweed trembling in
    the shallows
The final scream of a seabird celebrating
    the night
As I caress you and love you
    And lose myself in the spiritual mystery of
        night, the endless ocean—and you.

Years Have Slipped By

Years have slipped by, the good and painful ones
    as well,
    But what we are today is all that matters.
Know, my darling, that I am here for you, that
    your pain is mine,
    Your joy is mine as well.
More than anything in the world I want to know
    that
    I add to your happiness,
That I give you a fuller and more exciting life than
    You could ever have without me.
All I ask is you—your love, your trust, your
    caring—
    And that together in our love,
It will have made a difference that you and I
    Walked this earth together.

I Will Find You

I will find you even as I discover myself,
Find you if I must tour each continent, knock on
    doors,
      Explore ruins or sift through remote deserts.
I will find you with enough love to nurture me
    back
      To courage and understanding, joy and energy,
And a future that sings with hope and passion.
I have been alone long enough,
      Docile and speechless, lost and afraid.
I expect no miracle, no lightning bolt or comet
      Acclaimed in all corners of the world.
I just want someone free enough to love and be
    loved,
      To cling and to hold, to nourish and ask
        nothing
But love and commitment and mutual support.
I have struggled long enough, prayed patiently
        enough,
      Hidden silently enough.
Now I will reveal myself like a tree in all its
    seasons,
And love you, just love you, beyond logic and
    reasons.

It's Time

It's time to clothe my dreams in reality,
To create a home for wanderers
Who cannot bow before the traditions of a single-
    family dwelling
And a fenced-in yard.
Who look beyond marriage and blood
To gather brothers and sisters tied by more than
    custom and umbilical cords.
Generous minds and loving hearts,
    laughing eyes and simple tastes,
Who know that serenity at sunrise and peace at
    sunset
Are worth more than the treasuries of kings and
    IRA security.

It's time to clothe my dreams in reality
    To gather together kindred spirits
    Who look beyond what is and was
        To understand what can be,
    Who know that love and compassion, joy and
        peace are our birthright
    Stolen by a culture's madness and to band
        together the manipulations of frightened
        lives,
        wise minds and bruised hearts,
    Daring souls and brave spirits
    Who know that love is worth the stars
    And friendship does not hide its private
        anxieties behind sophistication and steel
    symbols.
It's time to clothe my dreams in reality
To move beyond jealousy and possession,
    isolation and imprisonment,
To confront boredom and loneliness,
    sadness and lovelessness
To make known my secret needs and reveal my
    hidden yearnings,
To risk self-exposure as the only path to final
    freedom
To surround myself with the energy flowing from
    the earth's core,
The passion of rivers and the resilience of trees,
And thus to clothe my dreams in reality!